THE ABDUCTION PREVENTION LIBRARY™

WHAT TO DO IF YOU GET LOST

Cynthia MacGregor

The Rosen Publishing Group's
PowerKids Press™
New York

Published in 1999 by The Rosen Publishing Group, Inc.
29 East 21st Street, New York, NY 10010

First Edition

Book Design: Danielle Primiceri

Photo Credits: All photo illustrations by Seth Dinnerman.

MacGregor, Cynthia.
      What to do if you get lost / by Cynthia MacGregor.
            p.   cm. — (The abduction prevention library)
      Includes index.
      Summary: Discusses the steps to follow when lost in order to get help.
      ISBN 0-8239-5250-9
      1. Safety education—Juvenile literature. 2. Children—Life skills guides—Juvenile literature.
      3. Self-reliance in children—Juvenile literature. [1. Lost children. Safety.]
      I. Title. II. Series.
HQ770.7.M3   1998
613.6—dc21   97–49268
                                                                                      CIP
                                                                                       AC

Manufactured in the United States of America

Contents

Erik

Erik walks to and from school every day with his friend Bobby. Their parents helped them plan out a safe route to and from school. Erik and Bobby take that route every day. But one day Bobby stayed home sick. So Erik asked his mom to pick him up from school.

That afternoon, Erik waited for his mom. He saw Seth, the school bully. Seth grabbed Erik's schoolbooks and ran away. Erik chased Seth, but Seth got away. Suddenly Erik realized he had run far from school. Erik was lost. He didn't know where he was or what to do.

◀ *Being lost can make you feel confused and sometimes a little scared.*

Marie Gets Lost

Marie thought she would never get lost. When she went outside to play, she always stayed on her block. She didn't walk to school. Instead, she rode the bus to school every day.

But one day Marie went to a big store with her mom. Marie saw a shirt that she liked and stopped to look at it. When she turned around, her mom was gone. Marie didn't know where her mom was.

Marie was lost.

Would you know what to do if you got lost like Marie?

Everyone has gotten lost at one time or another. Would you know what to do if it happened to you? ▶

Keep Calm

No matter where you get lost, there will be someone around who can help you. Most people will be happy to help you. But if someone makes you feel uncomfortable, walk away from that person and ask someone else. It's easy to get upset when you are lost. But try to stay calm and don't **panic** (PAN-ik). This will help you ask the right people for help. Staying calm will help you to think clearly and find a good place to get help.

Staying calm is the first step towards finding someone to help you when you are lost.

Stay Smart

If you get lost, it's important to stay smart. Be **aware** (uh-WAYR) of what's going on around you. This will help to keep you safe until you find your way home or back to your mom or dad.

If you were with someone when you got lost, like your mom or another grown-up, stay where you are. That person might be able to **retrace** (re-TRAYS) her steps and find you. If she doesn't find you in a few minutes, look for help. But if you weren't with someone or are in a place that feels unsafe, look for help right away.

Waiting in the same place where you last saw your dad or mom will help him or her to find you. ▶

Looking for Help

Looking for help means going to an area where there are people around. If you are in a store, for example, you can ask someone who works there to help you. But what if you are lost on a quiet street? Did you pass a street with more people on it before you got lost? Go back to that street. Next, it's important to find the right person to ask for help.

Who Do I Ask?

The best person to ask for help is a police officer. If you can't find a police officer, the next best person is a crossing guard. If you can't find a crossing guard, look for a woman who has kids with her. Or you can go into a store and ask a person who is working there for help. You can also use a **pay phone** (PAY FOHN) to call for help.

A woman with kids is a smart choice to ask for help. ▶
She will understand that being lost can be scary.

Emergency Money

You should always carry **emergency** (ee-MER-jen-see) money with you so you can make a phone call. How much does it cost to use a pay phone? If it costs 25 cents, always carry a quarter with you. If it is 35 cents, always carry a quarter and a dime. Then you can call home or your parent's office or a neighbor.

Remember that a call to 911, the emergency number, is always free. You can dial 911 and say "Help, I'm lost." Someone on the other end will be able to find out where you are and help you.

◀ *Always carry emergency money plus a little extra. Remember only to use it for emergencies!*

Calling 911

There are three reasons why it's smart to call 911 if you're lost and no one is able to help you.

✋ The number is easy to remember.

✋ The call is free. You can call if you forget your emergency money.

✋ The person who answers will be able to help you, because he or she will probably know where you are. If you're lost, you may not know what street you're on. But most 911 operators can tell where your call is coming from.

911 operators have a special map that tells them where you're calling from. ▶

What You Need to Know

Whether you call for help from a pay phone or ask someone for help, you should know a few things ahead of time:

👋 Your parents' names. You call them Mom and Dad, but what are their real names? Do either of them have a different last name than you? You should know that too.

👋 Your address.

👋 Your phone number.

👋 Your mom's or dad's phone number at work.

👋 The number of a relative or a neighbor whom you can call if you can't reach your parents.

◀ *You can write your important phone numbers on paper or cards that will fit in your pocket.*

Everyone Gets Lost

Everyone gets lost at one time or another. Did you know that even grown-ups get lost sometimes? It's true! So remember: Just because you might get lost doesn't mean that you are a bad or stupid person. Being aware and remembering the tips in this book will help you get to a safe place, or help someone to find you!

Glossary

aware (uh-WAYR) Knowing what is going on around you.

emergency (ee-MER-jen-see) A sudden need for quick action.

panic (PAN-ik) A very strong fear of something.

pay phone (PAY FOHN) A public phone that you put money into before you can use it.

retrace (re-TRAYS) To go back over something.

Index